The Three Pigs Build a House

Story by Carmel Reilly

Illustrations by Cesar Samaniego

The Three Pigs Build a House

Text: Carmel Reilly
Publishers: Tania Mazzeo and Eliza Webb
Series consultant: Amanda Sutera
  Hands on Heads Consulting
Editor: Gemma Smith
Project editor: Annabel Smith
Designer: Jess Kelly
Project designer: Danielle Maccarone
Illustrations: Cesar Samaniego
Production controller: Renee Tome

NovaStar

ISBN 978 0 17 033396 2

Cengage Learning Australia
Level 5, 80 Dorcas Street
Southbank VIC 3006 Australia
Phone: 1300 790 853
Email: aust.nelsonprimary@cengage.com

For learning solutions, visit **cengage.com.au**

Printed in China by 1010 Printing International Ltd
1 2 3 4 5 6 7 28 27 26 25 24

*Nelson acknowledges the Traditional Owners and Custodians
of the lands of all First Nations Peoples. We pay respect
to Elders past and present, and extend that respect to
all First Nations Peoples today.*

Contents

Chapter 1

Up on the Hill

Petula, Paddy and Piper Pig lived with their mum in a tiny house by a river.

One day, Mum said, "This house is much too small for all of us now. It's time for you three to get a place of your own."

"But where will we go?" asked Paddy.

"Why don't we build a house?" said Piper, excitedly. "There is spare land up on the hill."

The three pigs walked up the hill to look at the land.

"This is such a great spot!" said Petula.

"Yes, but what will we build our house out of?" asked Paddy.

Just then, a farmer came by.

"I've got all this straw I don't need," he said.

"Could you use it?"

"I think we could!" said Piper.

The pigs took the straw from the farmer.

Chapter 2

Making a New Home

The three pigs spent the next day planning their new home.

They watched several Do-View videos about building houses with straw.

"Are you sure your house will be strong enough?" asked Mum.

"Adding mud to the straw will make it strong," replied Piper.

"It's going to be amazing!" said Petula.

It only took the pigs a few hours to make the straw house.

They had just finished when there was a knock at the door.

Their mum had told the pigs never to let strangers into their home. So, they peered out the window to see if it was someone they knew.

"Who are you?" asked Piper.

"I'm Mr Wolf," said the stranger.
"And I want to come in to –"

"Come in?" said Paddy. "I'm sorry, we don't know you, so we can't let you in!"

Mr Wolf looked annoyed.

"If you don't let me in," he said,
"I will have no choice but to huff and puff
and blow your house down!"

"You can't do that!" said Piper.

"Oh, yes I can," said Mr Wolf,
taking a deep breath.

As he blew out, he set off a fierce wind.
In a few seconds, the whole house
had disappeared.

Paddy, Petula and Piper squealed in fright.

"Stop!" yelled Mr Wolf, as the pigs ran off.
"You need to –"

But the pigs were running too fast to hear
what he said.

Chapter 3

House Number Two

Back at Mum's house, the pigs told her what had happened.

"It wasn't just the wind that blew it down?" she asked.

"No!" said the pigs.

"Well, you definitely need to make a stronger house next time," said Mum. "I have some wood in the shed that will make a nice, solid home."

The three pigs built their new house quickly. They had just moved in when there was a knock at the door.

Mr Wolf was outside. "I need to come in and look around," he said.

"After what you did to our other house!" cried Piper. "Why would we let you in?"

Mr Wolf let out a loud sigh.
"You give me no choice," he said.
"If you don't let me in,
I'll have to huff and puff again."

"You'll never be able to blow this house down!" scoffed Petula.

Seconds later, after a fierce puff,
bits of wood and sticks flew into the air.

"I don't believe it!" squealed Paddy,
as the pigs turned and ran.

The pigs ran until they reached the river.

"I don't understand why that Mr Wolf is so mean," said Petula.

"Whatever the reason is," said Piper, "we need to build something *really* strong that he can't ever blow down."

Petula looked over to the water.
"Stones!" she said.

"We could make a solid house with those,"
said Paddy.

Chapter 4

A Solid House

It took the pigs a few weeks to build the stone house.

Mr Wolf arrived shortly after they had finished. "Hello!" he called.

The pigs looked down from the upstairs balcony. "You again!" cried Piper. "Well, you're not going to huff and puff and blow *this* house down!"

"No, I'm not," said Mr Wolf. "This place looks very solid. You three have learned a lot from building the other houses. I'm sure this one will meet city council standards."

"What do you mean?" asked Paddy.

Mr Wolf sighed. "I'm the Fairy Tale
Kingdom Council building inspector,"
he said. "I kept trying to tell you,
but you kept running off.
I'm surprised you didn't notice my
uniform or the sign on my car."

The pigs peered down at the car
parked outside.

"Oh, dear!" said Petula.

"My job is to check that new houses are
well made and safe," Mr Wolf added.
"I was hired for my great set of lungs.
They are the best safety test of all!"

The pigs came downstairs and let
Mr Wolf inside.

"You've done a fantastic job on this one,"
said Mr Wolf, looking around.

"However, I would suggest getting
a back door," he added with a smile.
"Just in case you ever need to make
a quick escape!"